The Honorary Treasurer's Handbook:

A Guide to Strengthening Financial Accountability

By Les Jones and
Tesse Akpeki

Sponsored by

Acknowledgements

The authors would like to acknowledge the following people, each of whom were generous with their support, expert advice and hard work: Professor Paul Palmer, David Taylor, Andrew Hind and Nigel Davies of the Charity Commission, Catherine Wood, Ben Kernighan of NCVO, Dorothy Dalton, Leonie Benton and Stuart Shariff of CASS Business School, UBS, the Honorary Treasurers Forum and the Charity Finance Directors Group.

Contents

Forewords

Andrew Hind, Chief Executive, Charity Commission

There is a strategic link between governance and finance and Honorary Treasurers are key players in promoting good governance in their charities. By strengthening the board of trustees' understanding of finance and supporting this group's ability to make financial decisions, Treasurers establish a sound basis for good governance. Standing alongside *Good Governance: A Code for the Voluntary and Community Sector*, the Honorary Treasurer's Handbook is a timely book that places the Treasurer in the broader context of good practice in trustee board governance.

The handbook explores the key relationships with the Chair, Chief Executive and Director of Finance, and both internal and external audit. Of value to both large and smaller charities alike, with a systematic approach and a wealth of practical advice, it demystifies and identifies the key aspects of the role. It demonstrates how the Honorary Treasurer can be instrumental in raising the financial awareness and ability of the whole board, thereby contributing to the effective and efficient delivery of a charity's mission and objectives.

With the role of charitable activity in wider society under active debate, never has the question of financial accountability been more important to voluntary sector organisations. The new climate of transparency and the call for ever higher standards in public life mean that all organisations, regardless of size or income, need to be able to answer for their financial conduct.

Trustee boards now need to hone their financial acumen and this handbook is a valuable resource to help achieve that aim.

Andrew Hind

David Rowe, Head of Charities, UBS Wealth Management UK

Charities are increasingly being called upon to take a bigger role in our society. The accountability of charities is widely debated and charities are expected to discharge their affairs competently and professionally. Some question whether voluntary charity trustees should even exist. We are of the firm belief that a voluntary ethos is fundamental to the charity sector. Supporting trustees and providing enabling services is core to UBS's philosophy of working with charities. We were therefore delighted when some three years ago, David King, the Honorary Treasurer of NCVO and Professor Paul Palmer approached UBS with a vision of an association for Honorary Charity Treasurers. We subsequently became and continue to be the lead sponsor of the Honorary Treasurer's Forum.

Regular meetings occur at the Cass Business School in the City of London, chaired by Bruce Gordon. At these meetings, Honorary Treasurers hear from experts on topical issues and are also able to network and share issues of both concern and success. Out of this has evolved this publication, *The Honorary Treasurer's Handbook*, undoubtedly the authoritative text on the roles and responsibilities of the charity Honorary Treasurer.

This publication, however, goes beyond being just a checklist of good practice. It provides sensible and practical advice on some of the thorny and difficult management issues which Honorary Treasurers face. The role of the Treasurer can, in many respects, be a lonely role. The Treasurer is jointly liable with his (or her) fellow trustees, but is also a first amongst equals when it comes to finance. He has a leadership role to fellow trustees, who look to him for guidance on financial issues. He also has, unlike other trustees an important relationship with the Director of Finance, which requires careful management, as the Treasurer is not this professional's line manager. That is the responsibility of the charity's Chief Executive.

As investment managers to around 500 charities with some £3 billion pounds of charity assets under management in aggregate, we regularly meet Honorary Treasurers and Finance Directors. Whether a small or large charity, we have observed one consistent element that ensures the success of a charity's financial performance – that is the Treasurer and Finance Director speaking with a united voice. Clear leadership and professional instruction, for example, enables us as investment managers to do our job, which is to get the best return for a given level of risk for our clients.

We are therefore very proud at UBS to have seen our investment grow and prosper for the good of the entire charity sector, and we offer our total support to the Honorary Treasurer's Forum and NCVO with this publication.

David Rowe

Bruce Gordon, Chairman, Honorary Treasurers Forum

I was very pleased when the Honorary Treasurers Forum was created a few years ago. As a serving Honorary Treasurer of a large charity I had felt for some time that there was a definite gap in the market for a forum that would allow Honorary Treasurers to network and share and resolve common problems. Treasurers have distinct and important roles to play in their charities and we need all the help we can get.

Since its inception, the Forum has developed well and I am very pleased and honoured to be its Chairman. The Forum meets regularly and occasionally contributes to the debate on important policy issues. It is great to talk to fellow Treasurers on a regular basis. During our discussions we identified another gap in the market: there was no definitive document that defined the role of Honorary Treasurer and the Forum was determined to ensure one was produced. I am delighted that this publication has been endorsed by the Charity Finance Directors Group (CDFG) and the Charity Commission. The end product is this publication, which we hope will assist all Honorary Treasurers in carrying out the very important work they perform.

I very much hope Honorary Treasurers and other interested parties will find this publication helpful and will enjoy reading it.

Bruce Gordon

Introduction

Finance is a primary concern for the leadership of voluntary and community sector organisations (VCOs) today. This is not really news: mission success has always depended on having adequate resources and using them effectively. Chief Executives, staff members and trustee boards have always sweated over budgets and struggled to stretch available funds to meet organisational needs. And, in its governance role, the board has always borne the daunting responsibility of providing financial oversight and security for the organisation.

Today, however, the challenge of finance seems to be growing. In addition to the many regulatory complexities facing VCOs, there is an emerging demand for greater accountability and transparency. Media coverage and more rigorous standards of reporting mean that practices that might have once been kept within the walls of the organisation are open to public scrutiny. The online databases, GuideStar and the Summary Information Return (SIR), make it easy for anyone to compare the financial performance of different organisations – sometimes to the organisations' cost. Add to this a volatile environment, where funders and the Government are radically revamping their ways of providing resources, and you have a very challenging situation for voluntary sector leaders indeed.

Not surprisingly, many organisations are actively looking for ways to strengthen financial effectiveness. And, because financial stewardship is at bottom a strategic governance issue, the best place to begin improving practice is in the boardroom. A financially savvy board asks the right questions, monitors the appropriate controls and understands the relationship between finance and strategic aims. It provides leadership and oversight in proper amounts, supports its executive financial staff and keeps the organisation on track and safe from risk. But how can organisations strengthen the relationship between governance and finance? How can they improve board engagement in financial matters?

Hidden treasure

One key lies in the figure of the Honorary Treasurer. Treasurers are financially skilled trustees charged with additional responsibility of guiding and advising the board as it carries out its duty of oversight. Although frequently undervalued, this is a pivotal role in any organisation, providing a vital interface between the work of the executive and the work of the governing body. Acting on behalf of the board, the Treasurer has the power to strengthen oversight, ensure accountability and improve the quality of financial stewardship at the governance level.

The Honorary Treasurer's Handbook provides a concise overview of the role of Treasurer, placing this skilled board officer in a governance context and defining his/her legal and ethical responsibilities to fellow trustees and to the organisation. Its practical approach will benefit newly appointed Treasurers as well as experienced Treasurers looking for ways to improve their effectiveness. Chairs, trustees, Chief Executives and Directors of Finance – anyone seeking to strengthen financial practice – will find the Handbook a mine of useful information, tips and techniques for making more of the Treasurer's role.

And the Handbook goes farther, offering a new approach to the Treasurer's role that unlocks its hidden potential. Beyond ensuring regulatory compliance and acting as the board's financial watchdog, the Treasurer can play an important role in developing board effectiveness. With increasing regulation and an escalating number of complex financial decisions to make, boards need a capable Treasurer to help them understand the connection between financial choices and mission success. Although the Director of Finance provides raw financial information, the Treasurer has the power to interpret the numbers and explain what they mean to programmes and services. Trusted, influential, skilled and always dedicated to the mission, the Treasurer is in a unique position to help trustees improve their financial competence and decision-making ability.

By strengthening and supporting the Treasurer, organisations enable this individual to strengthen and support the board in turn. This makes the Treasurer a key figure in empowering boards to provide the kind of leadership and financial oversight organisations so badly need. Although most organisations have a Treasurer, many fail to see this officer for what he or she really is: a potential resource for improving the quality of governance. The Honorary Treasurer's Handbook provides practical strategies for revealing this hidden treasure.

Contents

The first step to effectiveness in any position is establishing role clarity. The first chapter, The role of the Honorary Treasurer, gives guidelines on how the trustee board can frame the Treasurer's role to maximise its effectiveness. Model role descriptions and person specifications provide a starting point for organisations in the process of establishing their own guiding documents for the Treasurer's position. And, because a clear distinction between the roles of Treasurer and Director of Finance (DOF) is essential, this chapter also includes a model job description for the DOF.

Good organisational systems go a long way toward creating a climate where a Treasurer can succeed. Support for the role of Treasurer provides guidelines for establishing Treasurer selection criteria, identifying the best candidates for the position and providing the support they need once they take up the post. Once in position, the Treasurer must be able to work with a whole range of individuals and groups including the Director of Finance, key committees, the Chair and the board. Working effectively with others gives detailed guidelines on ways to establish good working practices with these partners and more.

The role of the Honorary Treasurer

The Honorary Treasurer plays an important, but often unsung, role in the life of any voluntary sector organisation. He or she is primarily a trustee with all the duties and obligations of any trustee plus a raft of additional responsibilities whose purpose is to help the trustee board to fulfil its obligation to provide financial oversight for the organisation. In the words of the Charity Commission:

'The Honorary Treasurer provides financial information to the trustees and maintains accounting standards. S/he may act as an "interpreter" for trustees who have little understanding of financial affairs so they can make informed decisions.'

An accurate description, however the role is broader than this. Although advising fellow trustees is a key skill, greater insight is needed into the complexity of the Honorary Treasurer's role in many organisations and the wide variance between the work Honorary Treasurers do in different kinds of organisations. For example, in many small organisations and in some medium-sized organisations, the Treasurer has a hands-on role. This means getting involved in the actual preparation of the budget and accounts, the authorisation of expenditure and cheque signing and so on. He or she may also be involved in setting the strategic agenda and projecting the financial impact of organisational strategies.

In larger organisations, the Treasurer is typically much less involved in day-to-day matters but needs to have a full appreciation of the finance and internal control environment as well as a thorough understanding of the finances of the organisation its strategies, budgets and so on. He or she works closely with the Director of Finance (DOF) and plays a vital role in keeping the trustee board briefed on what can be very complex financial information.

Main responsibilities: an overview

Trustee obligations
The Treasurer is first and foremost a trustee. This means that he or she has all the obligations of any trustee to uphold the terms of the governing document and act in the interests of the organisation. Like any trustee, the Treasurer must strive to support the organisation's mission, vision and values in all s/he does. S/he must participate fully in all trustee activities and abide by any codes of conduct or other policies she signed up to when she became a trustee.

Understanding the organisation's finances
The Treasurer must develop an understanding of the organisation's finances both in broad terms and in detail. This responsibility calls for financial skill and prior experience, qualities that usually distinguish the capable

Treasurer. In many cases, it also means being able to communicate effectively with the Chief Executive, Director of Finance, or other professional staff to share information. Additionally, the Treasurer must be able to understand financial questions from a strategic standpoint: that is, to see them from the governance perspective rather than from a managerial point of view.

Keeping up with regulation and reporting

The Treasurer needs to keep abreast of regulation and reporting obligations for the organisation. This means maintaining an awareness of what is happening in the sector through publications, email updates, networking, conferences and the like. Keep in mind that many kinds of regulations have financial implications for organisations, not only those that are strictly financial. Health and safety, taxation, and Criminal Records Bureau checks for personnel are all examples of areas where recent regulation calls for a response from organisations and should be monitored by the Treasurer.

Advising the trustee board

This responsibility lies at the heart of the Treasurer's role. Because of his/her special skill in financial matters, he/she has been chosen by the board to be their interpreter and guide. In this role the Treasurer will present and explain information to the board, offer an independent opinion, and advise on a course of action. S/he may go farther, working with trustees to develop their financial skills, such as how to read an annual report. And the Treasurer will work with the Chair and the Chief Executive to identify development opportunities for trustees that will strengthen their effectiveness in managing the organisation's finances as well as their strategic engagement.

Serving on key committees

The Treasurer is a necessary member of important committees such as the audit, finance, fundraising and investment committees. S/he can act for the board in setting up terms of reference and briefs for these committees. As committee Chair, s/he leads the work of the group and reports findings back to the trustee board. As a member, s/he represents the board's financial interests in debate and brings the mission into all discussions.

Working with the DOF and other staff

As the board advisor in financial matters, the Treasurer must maintain good working relations with various members of staff, particularly the DOF or Chief Financial Officer. S/he must be able to communicate effectively, acting as a medium for information between staff and the trustee board.

Communicating on behalf of the board

In many organisations the Treasurer has a visible role and acts as spokesperson for the trustee board on financial decisions. S/he may appear at the AGM and address members or work with fundraisers, speaking to funders about the organisation from a financial standpoint.

Defining the Treasurer's role: a job for the trustee board

To be effective, the Honorary Treasurer needs a clear understanding of his or her role. Role definition is fundamental to Treasurer recruitment and training, as well as to his or her working relationship with others in the organisation, especially the Director of Finance.

The trustee board is responsible for defining the role of the Honorary Treasurer. This guide contains information to help boards understand the role and initiate the discussion about what the Treasurer should do in their organisation. A board self-assessment or skill survey can help the group achieve focus. Once the board has determined what they need from their Treasurer, they must create a written job description and person specification for the role of Treasurer. Models for these documents are included in the following section.

For organisations that have a Director of Finance, it's essential that this executive role is coordinated with the non-executive role of the Honorary Treasurer. To achieve this, each role should have its own job description and person specification and these should give clear guidance in areas where there may be ambiguity between the two. A model job description for the DOF is included for comparison among the model documents.

Short form Treasurer's job description
Prepared by Les Jones

Purpose
To monitor the financial matters of the organisation and report to the board of trustees at regular intervals on its financial health in line with good practice and in accordance with the governing document and legal requirements. To oversee arrangements for risk management and ensure that these are adequate to organisational needs, governance requirements and legal obligations.

Trustee responsibilities
The Honorary Treasurer will fulfil all the duties, obligations and responsibilities of a trustee. In addition, he or she is authorised by the trustee board to carry out additional duties as described below.

Main responsibilities
- To oversee and present budgets, accounts and financial statements to the board of trustees;
- To ensure that proper accounts and records are kept, ensuring financial resources are spent and invested in line with good governance, legal and regulatory requirements;
- To be instrumental in the development and implementation of financial reserves and investment policies;
- To oversee major contracts including public service delivery commitments.

Main duties
- Liaising, where applicable, with the appropriate member of staff responsible for the financial activities of the organisation;
- Chairing any finance committee in line with standing orders and terms of reference, and reporting back to the board of trustees;
- Monitoring and advising on the financial viability of the organisation;
- Implementing and monitoring specific financial controls with effective systems in place;
- Advising on the financial implications of the organisation's strategic plan;
- Overseeing the organisation's management of risk process;
- Acting as a counter signatory on cheques and important applications to funders.

Treasurer's job description
Adapted for this publication from the Charity Finance Yearbook
by Les Jones

Trustee responsibilities
The Honorary Treasurer will fulfil all the duties, obligations and responsibilities of a trustee. In addition, he or she is authorised by the trustee board to carry out additional duties as described below.

Duties toward the board
- To guide and advise fellow trustees on the finance sub-committee and/or the trustee board in the approval of budgets, accounts and financial statements;
- To inform the trustee board about its financial duties and responsibilities and to assist in developing their financial skills and understanding;
- To advise on the financial implications of the organisation's strategic plans and key assumptions in the operational plan and budget, especially those outside the agreed boundaries of management authority;
- To ensure the development of an appropriate reserves policy and to provide assurance that the financial resources of the organisation meet its present and future needs;
- To ensure the development of an appropriate investment policy; to ensure that there is no conflict between investments held and the organisation's aims and values;
- To ensure the establishment of an adequate system of internal financial controls and to monitor its implementation and effectiveness;
- To monitor the organisation's investment activity and ensure its consistency with policy as well as with legal responsibilities;
- To develop financial skill and expertise on the board and among trustees.

Legislation and reporting
- To ensure the organisation's compliance with financial legislation;
- To ensure that accounts are prepared and disclosed in accordance with the requirements of statutory bodies and funders, reviewed or audited as required, and that audit recommendations are implemented.

Other duties

- To work in close co-operation with the Director of Finance (DOF), and provide support and advice to the organisation's staff and/or volunteers;
- To understand the accounting procedures and key internal controls which are in place, in order to be able to assure the board of the organisation's financial integrity;
- To ensure that equipment and assets are adequately maintained and insured;
- To develop a meaningful management accounts pack, in co-operation with the DOF, and to present to the finance sub-committee and/or to the trustee board;
- To meet the external and/or internal auditor independently of the DOF, at least annually;
- To advise and guide the organisation when it appoints the DOF.

Communicating

- To make a formal presentation of the accounts at the AGM, drawing attention to any important points in a coherent and easily understandable way;
- To contribute to the organisation's fundraising strategy (if relevant);
- To sit on appraisal, recruitment and disciplinary panels, as required.

Treasurer's person specification

In addition to the general person specification required of any trustee, the Treasurer should have the following characteristics:

- Financial experience
- Financial qualifications desirable (for larger organisations)
- Experience of organisation finance, fundraising and pension schemes (as relevant)
- Experience in budget setting and monitoring
- Experience working in the voluntary sector
- Knowledge of the sector's reporting regime
- Ability to present financial information clearly, and make it understandable for non-finance people
- The skills to analyse proposals and examine their financial consequences
- The skills to manage change
- The skills to analyse and interpret financial data
- Willingness and approachability to deal with enquiries from trustees and staff on an ad hoc basis

Director of Finance Job Description
Prepared by Andrew Hind for the Charity Finance Yearbook

Primary objective
Provide sound financial advice to trustees, the Chief Executive and other senior management colleagues. Provide an effective financial management service to the charity or voluntary or community sector organisation (VCO) and its subsidiary companies, if any. Act as the leading interface between management and trustees on financial matters.

Reports to: Chief Executive

Specific duties
- Ensure, in close cooperation with the Chief Executive and Honorary Treasurer, that an appropriate financial policy framework is in place to guide the charity's/VCO's financial decision making. In particular, clarity will be required on reserves, expense ratios and income mix questions;
- Ensure the appropriateness of the key assumptions included in the charity's/VCO's medium term financial plan and annual budget proposals. Provide advice to senior management colleagues and trustees on these matters;
- Contribute to the preparation of the charity's/VCO's strategic plan. Prepare the annual budget and forecasts;
- Advise the Honorary Treasurer and other trustees on major financial issues which arise and which are outside the agreed boundaries of management authority, for example, a proposed major new fundraising initiative or a contract for service provision;
- Service the trustees' audit committee;
- Maintain regular liaison with the Honorary Treasurer;
- Work closely with the Chief Executive, the director of the charitable service department and the fundraising director as part of a mutually supportive senior management team;
- Advise all three on the likely financial consequences of all proposed courses of action;

- Maintain records to meet legal and tax requirements and to measure both the inputs and the outcomes of the charity's/VCO's operations. Provide accounting services for use by managers in planning and controlling the work of the charity or VCO. This includes financial accounting, management accounting, forecasting, budgeting and control systems;
- Plan and manage the charity's/VCO's tax liabilities under existing and proposed legislation;
- Evaluate the tax liability impact of contemplated courses of action, minimise the tax burden and deal with tax authorities;
- Prepare the statutory annual accounts;
- Plan and manage cash flow and investment activity – the latter in consultation with investment advisers and the relevant trustee sub-committee, if any;
- Maintain contact with bankers, investment managers, pension advisers and auditors;
- In close consultation with the Chief Executive and Honorary Treasurer, establish a relationship with each trustee so that each individual has an opportunity to understand fully the key financial issues confronting the charity or VCO;
- Keep abreast of financial developments across the sector by liaising with senior finance staff in other charities and VCOs and contributing to the activities of the Charity Finance Directors' Group (CFDG).

Support for the role of Treasurer

Selecting a Treasurer

The selection of a Treasurer is a key decision for any trustee board. An important part of selection is knowing what you are looking for. An up-to-date job description and person specification, like the ones included in this publication, provide a starting point for the search. General characteristics to look for include:

Commitment to the organisation
The Treasurer's role is an important one. The person who undertakes it must always have the best interests of the organisation at heart.

Understanding of trusteeship
The Treasurer is always a trustee first. He or she needs to embrace the responsibilities of trusteeship and understand that the Treasurer only has the authority granted him/her by the trustee board. For more information on the duties of trusteeship, see CC3, The Essential Trustee, available from the Charity Commission.

Willingness to devote the necessary time and energy
The job of Treasurer is a big commitment. Organisations looking to appoint a new Treasurer need to provide a realistic sense of just how much time and energy the role will take. Prospective Treasurers need to understand the scope of their commitment when they take to role on.

Financial knowledge
Treasurers should ideally have finance knowledge and experience in dealing with the level of financial activity the organisation engages in. It isn't always strictly necessary for the Treasurer to be a trained accountant. For smaller organisations, some basic bookkeeping knowledge is adequate; for a larger organisation, greater expertise is needed. In large organisations, the Treasurer must be able to understand a full range of financial issues and be able to work credibly alongside professional financial staff, like the DOF, as well as auditors and consultants.

Leadership ability
The Treasurer is an important advisor to the board. S/he needs to have the trust and respect of this group in order to work with them effectively. Beyond this, the Treasurer must also be able to provide leadership for the board in financial matters. This may mean offering analysis, suggesting courses of action, introducing new ideas or championing new ways of doing things. A competent Treasurer will stick his or her neck out for something s/he feels strongly about.

Independence

A Treasurer needs good, independent judgement and must be willing to speak her/his mind. Sometimes s/he must make unpopular recommendations to the board and stand up for what may be controversial proposals. While not courting conflict, the Treasurer should have the confidence to hold a position under fire.

Strategic vision

The Treasurer's role is an important interface between management (the Chief Executive and the DOF) and the governing body. To be effective, the Treasurer needs to have a clear understanding of the difference between operational and strategic issues.

Ability to work with others

The Treasurer needs to be able to work with others as part of a team. He or she will work closely with the board, with the DOF and with the members of important committees such as the audit and investment committees. The Treasurer may also work with individuals from outside the organisation such as consultants, independent auditors, partners and funders. He or she may also be called on to work with staff members, providing information and advice when asked.

Special skills

If the organisation is involved in specialised activities, such as trading, the Treasurer needs some experience in these areas.

Treasurer recruitment

The Treasurer recruitment process is an important opportunity to bring needed skills into your organisation. Many organisations appoint their Treasurers on the recommendation of one or more of the existing trustees. This is fine provided the candidate meets the requirements of the job description. Some organisations advertise the Treasurer's role. Again, all serious candidates must meet the requirements of the job description and person specification authored by the trustee board.

Help in finding a Treasurer can be obtained by contacting the Charity Finance Directors Group (CFDF) and the Honorary Treasurers Forum. The Institute of Chartered Secretaries and Administrators (ICSA) can put potential Treasurers in touch with VCOs, as can networks of ethnic and minority financial professionals such as African and Caribbean Diversity (ACD). For addresses and contact details, see *Resources*.

Inducting a new Treasurer

Like anyone entering a new role, the Treasurer benefits from an induction. Even if he or she is a trustee of long-standing, a formal induction will help him or her be more effective. If the Treasurer is new to the organisation, s/he should go through a full trustee induction process first, and then tackle the task of learning the Treasurer's role. In all cases, the board should take time to establish an induction process that will give the new Treasurer necessary information quickly and efficiently.

To help the process along, the serving Treasurer should set aside time to go over the duties with the new appointee. In some organisations, the incomer spends a few months or weeks 'shadowing' the existing Treasurer, going where he goes and doing what s/he does in order to learn the ropes. The DOF also has a responsibility to help the new Treasurer learn his or her role. The trustee board should make it clear that the DOF needs to set aside time to meet with the new candidate and brief him/her on financial issues in the organisation. Other staff members such as fundraisers and trading division managers, as well as standing members of board committees, may also contribute to the induction of a new Treasurer.

Information for a new Treasurer

General information
- a complete overview of the Treasurer's role in the organisation including committee work, if any;
- an accurate estimate of the amount of time the Treasurer's role will require;
- a statement from the board on how it deals with finance from a governance perspective;
- a list of finance-related committees and a full schedule of their meetings;
- a schedule for management accounts plus a description of the Treasurer's role in their presentation to the board;
- a briefing on statutory accounts: did the auditors recommend the last ones without reservation?

Key documents
- a copy of SORP 2005, plus guidance notes from the Charity Commission;
- the Charity Commission publication CC61: Charity Accounts, the Framework;
- the organisation's current strategic plan;
- the organisation's fundraising and marketing plans;
- the organisation's risk policy, an overview of risks and associated information and internal financial controls;
- the details of pension schemes;
- a briefing on investment policy and procedures;
- an overview of trading projects and issues;
- statutory report and accounts timetable;
- Internal audit plan, if applicable.

Training for Treasurers

There are many opportunities for Treasurers to receive financial and other training, much of it free. The Charity Treasurers' Forum offers formal presentations on key issues plus networking opportunities. Many accounting firms large and small run low cost or free seminars for voluntary sector Treasurers. Contact your auditor, solicitor or investment manager to find out what services they offer or see the Charity Commission website for more information (www.charitycommission.gov.uk).

Working effectively with others

The board

The trustee board has the responsibility for overseeing the organisation's finances. To do this more effectively, it authorises the Treasurer to act on its behalf as advisor and guide in financial matters. The Treasurer's task is to prompt, coach and assist the board as it endeavours to understand important financial issues like the reserves policy, the key components of business or operational plan, the accounts, budget, systems and procedures risks. S/he helps the trustee board to build an overall picture of the organisation's true financial situation that will allow them to exercise responsible governance.

Developing the board's financial ability
The Treasurer, working with the Chair, can help improve the financial ability of individual trustees and of the board as a group.

Create a financial governance pack

The Treasurer can assemble a comprehensive financial governance pack for all trustees. This should form an important part of the induction pack offered to new trustees, but all trustees should receive one and be guided through its contents by the Treasurer or the DOF when appropriate.

The pack should include:
- a description of how financial governance works in the organisation including the role of the trustee board and all the relevant committees;
- a clear statement of the financial responsibilities that come with trusteeship;
- key board policies relating to finance and financial procedures and internal financial controls;
- a summary of more detailed financial policies like the reserves policy, the investment policy and other important documents;
- a list of the important financial committees and their members;
- the key dates in the annual financial cycle;
- the latest set of annual report and accounts;
- the most recent budget;
- an explanation of the scheme of financial delegation in the organisation.

Offer a short course in reading financial statements

Another simple way for the Treasurer to improve basic financial know-how on the board is to run a workshop on how to read and understand the financial statement. He or she should take time with trustees to explain this document in layperson's terms and show its relevance to the organisation's success. Trustees who require extra coaching should be able to seek out more help from the Treasurer as needed.

Build a climate of confidence

By building trustee confidence, the Treasurer can help create a climate where trustees feel they can ask financial questions. A respectful, helpful attitude toward the questions posed by non-experts can go a long way in encouraging useful exchange in the boardroom. In his or her work with the DOF, the Treasurer can encourage this executive to adopt a similar attitude of openness, approachability and respect.

Demystify finance language

The Treasurer can help trustees by providing jargon-free explanations of financial terms and procedures, giving them the vocabulary to discuss financial questions intelligently. He or she may prepare a short glossary of financial terms for other trustees to help them get to grips with the language. The Treasurer can also act as an interpreter for the DOF and the Chief Executive, helping translate their specialist language in to plain terms for the benefit of the other trustees.

Link mission, vision and finance

For the layperson, finance can often seem to exist in a world of its own, unrelated to mission aims or vision. The Treasurer can help the board by bridging the gap between the numbers and the real effects they have on the organisation's ability to fulfil its mission. By showing how financial realities affect such things as programmes and the future of the organisation, the Treasurer can help the board build its understanding of the link between finance, strategy and delivering services.

Recruit expertise

Working with the Chair, the Treasurer can be instrumental in persuading the board to recruit new members with financial expertise. He or she can contribute to creating the trustee job description and take part in the recruitment process in order help find the right individuals. The Treasurer should also take an active role in identifying and preparing his or her own replacement, thus ensuring the continuity of good financial support for the board.

Keep the board updated

A key task for the Treasurer is keeping the board abreast of the latest changes in regulations. Financial regulations are naturally on the top of the Treasurer's agenda, but Treasurers need to be aware that other kinds of regulation carry financial and risk implications for the organisation, too. These include health and safety, employment law, and contract law and taxation, among others.

The Treasurer should monitor changes to all areas that may have an impact on the financial or risk management activity of the organisation and prepare updates in plain terms for the benefit of fellow trustees. There are many sources of regulatory information available to Treasurers. A number of law and accountancy firms provide free updates online. For more complex issues, many of these firms also offer training for boards in all kinds of regulatory matters. The Charity Commission provides the latest in its regulatory changes on its website. For more information on receiving regulatory updates, see *Resources*.

Develop procedures for whistleblowing

Every organisation should have in place a whistleblowing policy and a confidential procedure that will allow whistleblowers to bring their concerns to the attention of the governing board. The Treasurer, a key figure in ensuring accountability, should make certain that whistleblowing policies and procedures are adequate. He or she should be on the team of trustees that deals with cases of whistleblowing. For advice on whistleblowing and establishing procedures, contact Public Concern at Work. See Resources for more details.

Advocate early filing

A quarter of voluntary sector organisations miss the deadline for filing, according to a recent Charity Commission survey, and many others just barely get their forms in on time. Yet the Honorary Treasurer should view timely filing as an important indicator of financial health and work toward making it happen. He or she can work with the board, the Chair and the DOF to make sure accounts are reviewed and signed off by the board in time to meet the deadline. Meeting the challenge may mean making changes to the organisation such as altering reporting patterns and changing the date of the AGM: the Treasurer can lend support to any measures that help the organisation meet its filing obligations. Refer to the Charity Commission's website for helpful information about the annual return and tips on planning the production of the report and accounts.

The Chair

The Treasurer should have a close and effective working relationship with the Chair. In some organisations the Treasurer is also the Deputy or Vice Chair. The Treasurer should meet with the Chair outside the main meetings to brief him or her on the financial issues that will be presented to the trustees. It will be particularly important that the Chair is fully briefed on important issues like the budget, the statutory accounts and important financial policies. In some organisations the Chair actually attends the finance committee.

The Treasurer should also ensure that there are no financial surprises for the Chair. At trustee meetings the Chair should allow the Treasurer to make any financial points he wishes to the trustees, guiding the board as they debate and make decisions on financial questions. The Chair should seek advice from the Treasurer about the organisation's plans in order to make sure that he or she is satisfied with the financial implications. The Treasurer's perspective should also be sought regarding specialist financial areas like investments and pensions.

The Chief Executive

The Chief Executive delegates responsibility for day-to-day financial management to the DOF and as such the DOF is the individual best placed to work with the Treasurer. It is however important that there is a good working relationship between the Treasurer and Chief Executive and that the two establish clear boundaries.

Some direct discussion between the Chief Executive and the Treasurer on financial matters should take place. To help both parties, many organisations draw up guidelines for the Chief Executive on how and when to work with the Treasurer. The two should meet at scheduled times during the year to discuss financial matters.

A survey of Chief Executives revealed their view of the most effective Treasurer activity:

- The Treasurer reviews management accounts on a quarterly basis (or monthly in unusual circumstances).
- In larger organisations, the Treasurer steers clear of involvement in day-to-day financial activities; these should be left to paid staff.
- The Treasurer looks at top line rather than detail.
- The Treasurer only monitors performance against strategy.
- The DOF has regular meetings with the Treasurer; the Chief Executive meets regularly with the Chair.
- Chief Executive only attends audit or finance committee meetings where there are specific issues.
- The DOF represents management at audit and finance committee meetings.
- The DOF should keep the Treasurer informed, meeting as often as necessary.

The Director of Finance (DOF)

The Treasurer and DOF need to have a close working relationship with the Treasurer skilfully playing the role of the very interested non-executive. They need to thoroughly discuss the ongoing management accounts, the budget, the statutory accounts and key financial policies.

The DOF needs to ensure that the Treasurer is kept informed on an ongoing basis albeit taking into account the executive/non-executive relationship. The DOF should ensure there are no surprises for the Treasurer.

Sometimes the Treasurer will need to act as the trustees' interpreter of key financial issues and policies which the DOF, being the technical expert, may not be able to do as simply as the Treasurer. This part of the Treasurer/DOF relationship can be skilfully promoted with the trustees to form an effective 'double act'.

Establishing a working agreement

Written working agreements are known to strengthen Chief Executive/Chair partnerships and they can help DOFs and Treasurers work together more effectively, too. Such an agreement can be drawn up by the Treasurer and the DOF on their own or working with the help of a trained facilitator or trusted third party. An agreement should cover:

- meeting times and places;
- important events on the reporting schedule;
- a code of personal conduct: How will they behave toward one another?
- communication guidelines;
- a clear breakdown of responsibilities: operational, strategic, governance;
- committee responsibilities (DOF and Treasurer should be jointly responsible for finance and audit committee meetings);
- special areas of activity, such as pensions;
- protocol for delivering joint reports to the board;
- protocol for contact including phone calls, emails and visits to the office by the Treasurer;
- protocol for requesting information or meeting with other staff or board members.

In the boardroom

It is vital that the Treasurer and the DOF are both fully briefed at board meetings and are seen to be working together. This is not to say that the Treasurer must agree with everything the DOF says: his or her role as 'critical friend' is vital to establishing accountable practices and a healthy interchange between the governing body and financial staff. The Treasurer and the DOF must work closely on board papers and committee reports in advance of meetings, addressing concerns beforehand. Both parties must be in possession of all relevant facts prior to the meeting and there should be no surprises for either party during the meeting.

Committee work

As Honorary Treasurer, committee work will form an important part of your duties. The Treasurer should be a member of all key financial committees, including finance, audit and investment committees. These small groups perform the vital service of overseeing financial activity in the organisation and advising the board. They may be made up of other trustees, staff members (especially the DOF) and advisors from outside the organisation. In some organisations the Treasurer will have the job of chairing financial committees.

To be effective, committees must be provided with a full written brief from the board that outlines their purpose, defines their membership and provides a framework for carrying out their work including meeting and reporting requirements. Additionally, any committee duties should be spelled out for the Treasurer in his or her job specification. Because the work of committees is often such an important part of the job, the Treasurer should receive an introduction to committee responsibilities as part of his or her induction.

Finance vs. audit committees

Finance committee: a small group including the Treasurer that takes charge of all financial matters including accounts, reporting and preparing financial information for presentation to the board.

Audit committee: a group that focuses specifically on the task of managing internal or external audits and risk management

The Treasurer is effective when...

You can tell when your Treasurer is really doing his/her job effectively when your organisation benefits from the following:

- The trustee board is interested and knowledgeable about organisational finances and discusses them enthusiastically.

- Finance is seen as a tool to good governance and management, not as an end in itself.

- The Treasurer can explain complex financial issues in a simple way to his/her trustee colleagues.

- Board and staff members are able to talk confidently about the relationship between financial accounts and activities and programmes.

- The organisation has an effective way of assessing and dealing with risk, particularly where internal controls are concerned.

- A complete system of internal controls is up and running.

- Strategic and operational plans are fully integrated with the budget.

- Statutory accounts and the trustees' annual report are clear, transparent and provide a real picture of what the organisation is achieving.

- The organisation files reports on time.

- External auditors approve the accounts with no qualification.

- The Treasurer has a very good working relationship with the DOF.

- The Treasurer has a very good working relationship with the Chair.

Taking action

When problems arise, the Treasurer needs to respond.

Problem: there is no regular financial reporting
Action: begin at once to establish a system

Problem: there has never been a regular system for reporting
Action: establish a system then launch a review process for past years to catch mistakes

Problem: the financial reporting schedule is breaking down; trustees are not receiving timely or accurate financial information
Action: investigate immediately and find out why it's happening, what needs to be done and how quickly the schedule can be re-established

Problem: the organisation's finances are deteriorating
Action: speak to the board immediately to make it understand the situation and take remedial action

Problem: a case of fraud has occurred
Action: carry out a full investigation, examine and report on the findings, suggest changes in policy to the board then monitor that the changes have been implemented on an operational level. Refer to the police as appropriate. Undertake legal proceedings when advisable.

Good practice notes on key areas

Working with SORP 2005 and SIR

SORP 2005

The Charity Commission's Statement of Recommended Practice 2005 (SORP 2005) is the key guidance document for all voluntary sector organisations. Introduced in 2005, it must be complied with for all financial year-ends beginning on or after the 1st of April 2005. It is therefore a very current challenge for organisations and their Treasurers.

SORP 2005 asks more of organisations in terms of information. It expands and improves the contents of the trustee report – an important area of influence for the Treasurer. Key to the new style of reporting is the inclusion of measured outputs, outcomes and impacts, achievements against objectives and future plans. Information needs to be directly relevant and all activities linked to the charitable aims of the organisation. New information about trustee recruitment and training must also be included.

SORP 2005 presents a challenge, but early adopters have found the new approach beneficial, providing a way to contextualise and evaluate organisational activity as well as financial information. It offers a more narrative approach to reporting that allows outsiders whether they are funders, service users or regulators, to form a clear picture of what your organisation does and how it is performing. Finally, its systematic approach to information can help organisations improve governance and the quality of financial oversight overall.

Treasurers can help their organisations by getting behind the changes needed to fulfil the obligations of the SORP 2005. They can support the new system by educating the board about the reasons behind the change, by assisting the DOF to collect information and by advocating early adoption and early filing.

A first step for Treasurers is to visit the Charity Commission's website and download a copy of SORP 2005 and the Commission's advice for implementation. The Commission also offers worked examples and packs for smaller charities in support of organisations adopting SORP 2005.

Charities registered and/or operating in Scotland and Northern Ireland need to be aware of any additional requirements concerning the preparation of the annual report and accounts and the audit requirements that may apply. Helpful information is available from the Office of the Scottish Charities Regulator and the Charities Branch of the Voluntary and Community Unit of the Social Development Directorate (Northern Ireland). See *Resources* for contact details.

The Summary Information Return (SIR)

The Summary Information Return (SIR) forms part of the Charity Commission's Annual Return requirement (Part C of the Annual Return). SIR is a requirement for organisations with an annual income of £1 million or more and represents a new initiative on the part of the Charity Commission to promote more transparency and accountability in the voluntary sector.

Inspired by the Prime Minister's Strategy Unit report 'Private Action, Public Benefit', and complementing GuideStar, the online database that delivers financial and performance information about nonprofit organisations in the USA, the SIR provides the Charity Commission with information to build its own online resource of information about the UK sector. This information is freely available to anyone wishing to access it via the Charity Commission website and will, over time, give a comparative picture of the performance of individual organisations and provide a source of information about the sector as a whole.

Treasurers can support SIR by helping their boards understand the value of such a resource. An attitude of openness and transparency reflects well on an organisation and inspires service users, members and funders with confidence. Additionally, organisations can benefit from SIR by using the online database to learn about other organisations and measure their strategic performance against sector-wide standards. A positive attitude on the part of the Treasurer – plus strong advocacy of timely filing – can help the organisation overcome anxiety about making its information public and profit from this innovative use of technology.

For more on SIR, including detailed guidance notes, see the Charity Commission's website www.charitycommission.gov.uk.

Budgeting and strategic planning

Budgeting and strategic financial planning are essential in all organisations, regardless of their size and should be part of the overall planning process in which the mission and long-term strategic goals of the organisation are affirmed (or amended) and short term objectives and SMART action plans (Specific, Measurable, Achievable, Realistic and Time-framed) which will deliver the goals are agreed. The budget should flow from this process as a financial representation of the organisation's operational plans for a given future period.

In a small organisation with no staff, the Treasurer will have a key role in the production of the financial budget. What can be lacking in this size of organisation is the formal review of direction and confirmation that the organisations activities remain consistent with its governing document. Incremental budgeting, based on last year's results with, perhaps, an allowance for inflation, can mean that the trustees fail to go back to first principles in considering the overall strategic plan, which can, over time, lead to drift from the stated objects of the organisation.

In larger organisations where there are paid financial staff it is difficult to be prescriptive about the trustees' role in the strategic financial planning process because organisations vary in size and in the experience and expertise of both staff and trustees. The questions organisations should ask are: first, whether current practices allow trustees to discharge their legal and fiduciary duties; and, second, whether both staff and trustee talents and resources are being used in the most effective way. There is a risk of an 'us and them' culture developing between staff and trustees if processes are not designed to build a constructive, mutually supportive partnership. The Treasurer may have an important role here in understanding the capabilities of the finance team and advising the trustees appropriately.

Furthermore, in order to prevent misunderstandings and bad feeling between staff and trustees, it is the role of trustees, advised by the Treasurer, to set the underpinning parameters and principles, and to then allow the paid staff to get on with building the detailed budget. The board needs to evaluate the budget according to how well it adheres to those underpinning parameters and not based on the detailed items within the budget.

Trustees should, however, be able to challenge any assumptions made by finance staff in the development of the budget. The board needs to be certain that it surveys each income and expenditure stream, and understands its risks and its significance to cash flow. Trustees may also wish to review the budget-building approach to make sure it's appropriate for the organisation.

- Zero-based budgeting, where the budget is built from scratch, is time consuming but may be best for new or changing income and expenditure streams.
- Incremental budgeting may be acceptable where it is clear that the income or expenditure stream is relatively static (for example, the fixed establishment costs of rent) and rates can be predicted fairly accurately using an incremental approach.
- Many organisations are now exploring new ways of budgeting, using activity based budgeting or the 'beyond budgeting' approach which focuses on target financial outputs rather than income and costs.

The trustee body, advised by the Treasurer, may wish to set limits on the day-to-day accounting procedures to limit exposure to risk, for example by requiring that income streams are received or at least legally guaranteed before making legal commitments for related expenditure.

To carry out his/her role effectively the Treasurer will need to be involved in developing both the plans and budgets and the underlying parameters that support them. Organisations should produce a strategic plan, an operating plan and of course, a budget. All these should be fully integrated and all should take into account the following:

- the external environment including the climate for competitor analysis and the general economic environment;
- the physical targets that the organisation wishes to achieve including outputs, outcomes and impacts. Whatever the state of existing measurement, plans and budgets should include physical targets;

- the overall financial position of the organisation including reserves, the cash position, the robustness of fundraising and income assumptions and so on;
- contracts and public service delivery agreements.

Management accounts

Having set the budget, good practice requires that the trustees monitor actual performance against the budget throughout the year. This is done through management accounts, a set of financial reports presented to the trustee board and senior management for review on a regular basis, normally quarterly or monthly.

The format of the basic management accounts is likely to be a report of actual results for the period and year to date compared to budgets for the same periods and with the variance between actual and budget calculated. Investment performance should be included, when appropriate. The report should also include the full year's budget and the latest forecast, when available. A forecast should be prepared and presented at least twice a year.

The board needs to decide what level of detail it requires and the Treasurer has an important advisory role to play in framing board requests for information. Normally, the board needs to see accounts at summary level only; that is, showing total income and expenditure for each major income stream and programme cost centre plus main support department cost centres. There should also be a balance sheet that shows movement and balances on unrestricted and restricted funds.

As part of this process it is also important for the Treasurer to understand the different funds, restricted, designated and unrestricted, which make up the organisation's assets, as it is essential that management accounts clearly differentiate between different funds.

Preparing accounts in small organisations
In a small organisations, the Treasurer may be directly involved in the preparation of the management accounts. He or she should work with the trustee board to establish what information they need to know in order to evaluate organisational performance and take necessary action. The accounts should be keyed into the strategic plan and the overall budget. The Treasurer should offer the board guidance as to the implications of the information.

In many organisations, accounts are presented as part of a pack of information that includes other documents to help trustees make sense of the financial information. These may include:

- a narrative of significant events in the period;
- an explanation of significant variances in the accounts;
- key performance indicators;
- graphical representation of key information;
- more detailed information on any areas of concern.

> **TIP** Presentation matters: all documents should be clearly written, easy to read and accompanied by good quality graphic material when possible. Consider asking for administrative support to improve the quality of management account information.

Preparing accounts in larger organisations

Where the organisation is large enough to employ finance professionals, the Treasurer's role is largely one of oversight. His or her contribution is as follows:

- to advise fellow trustees on the types of information which will be useful in managing the organisation;
- to work with the finance team to ensure that they understand what the trustees require and are able to provide it within the necessary timeframe;
- to liaise with the finance team once the information is prepared to ensure that the presentation is clear and that the Treasurer is in a position to answer any questions thrown up by fellow trustees;
- to place the accounts in context for fellow trustees, presenting them along with any additional information needed for the trustees to understand their implications for the organisation.

Where there is a problem in producing the information the trustees require, the Treasurer may need to investigate the underlying accounting systems or coding structures being used by the organisation and to work with the finance team to develop the available reporting. Staff have a responsibility to produce information required by the trustees in an understandable, accurate and timely fashion, but they may require the Treasurer's assistance in the first instance to achieve this. Establishing a deadline may speed the process: for example, requesting that management accounts be produced within seven days of the end of the reporting period.

Statutory reporting

On appointment, the Treasurer should use the updated publication CC61 *Charity Accounts: The Framework* and the Charity Commission's Statement of Recommended Practice 2005 (SORP) to determine the form of statutory reporting and the type of external review required by the organisation. There are a number of contributing factors including legal form, level of income and the content of the governing instrument that influence the requirements.

This exercise may, particularly in smaller organisations, show up previous bad practice, for example: accounts not in standard format as determined by the most recent Charity Commission statement of recommended practice (SORP 2005); inadequate trustees report; incorrect type of independent review etc. In this situation, the Treasurer should act sensitively to remedy the situation and educate fellow trustees in good practice. Wholesale change by the 'new broom' may cause ill feeling, and rejection of the changes.

Who undertakes the various tasks in preparing the statutory accounts will again depend on the level of skill within the organisation. Where there are professionally qualified staff, they should prepare the accounts, at least in draft, perhaps involving the Treasurer in a review at the draft stage. In other circumstances, the Treasurer may be required to prepare the end of year accounts, or it may be decided to outsource the task completely.

Remember that responsibility for the annual report and accounts rests with the trustee body as a whole, so it is essential that whole board feel ownership. One of the Treasurer's tasks is to 'guide and advise' fellow trustees in the approval of the accounts, so it is important for the Treasurer to be fully aware of their content, regardless of the level of involvement in their preparation. It is also important that the Treasurer can explain financial presentation and jargon to non-financial colleagues. Information should be presented to the board clearly, concisely and without jargon.

Statutory year-end accounts should be presented at the AGM. Incorporated organisations are legally required to circulate accounts 21 days before the AGM (ideally the same for unincorporated in order to provide sufficient time for review).

The statutory accounts should include a suitable reserves policy, investment policy, risk assessment statement and trustees report including a review of the year and future plans. These should be reviewed and agreed by all trustees. The Treasurer should sign the approved accounts on behalf of the board.

Serving on the audit committee

The audit committee monitors the organisation's financial reporting, reviews the internal financial control and risk management systems and considers the work of external auditors, including their independence, objectivity and effectiveness. Where applicable it also monitors and reviews the internal audit function. (See External audits and Internal audits for more information.) An area of increasing relevance and importance for audit committees is the need for proper policies and procedures to help prevent fraud and unethical activities. This is important particularly where reputation is key to success.

The audit committee is appointed by the board to act on its behalf and it reports back to the board in all matters. Logically, the Treasurer should serve on, if not lead, this committee. Its responsibilities, membership requirements, tenure and reporting duties must be laid out, in writing, in a detailed brief from the board. For an idea of how such a brief might look, see the sample terms of reference for an audit committee below.

In the private sector, audit committees should be made up of three independent non-executive directors, including one with recent and relevant financial experience. Their tenure should be for up to three years extendable by only two additional periods. The Higgs review states that as good practice the company secretary should act as secretary to the committee. These guidelines could well apply to large organisations.

In any case, all members of the audit committee must be well briefed on their own role and on the mission and strategy of the organisation. They need to keep up to date with changes in financial reporting requirements and in the regulatory framework (both the DOF and the Treasurer can help here). The DOF, head of internal audit (if any) and a representative of the external auditors should attend meetings at the invitation of the committee. The Chair, Chief Executive and other board members may be invited if appropriate. However, there should be at least one meeting a year where the external auditors attend without management present.

The audit committee should meet at least three times per year, more frequently if necessary. In medium sized organisations many matters relating to the audit committee will be covered in general board meetings, and the audit committee may only be required to meet twice a year when discussing the external or internal audit and accounts. However care should be taken in this case to ensure that the responsibilities of the audit committee are given sufficient attention.

Terms of reference for an audit committee
(used by permission of Dorothy Dalton)

Approved by the board of trustees on [date]

Overall responsibility
Take delegated responsibility on behalf of the board of trustees for ensuring that there is a framework for accountability; for examining and reviewing all systems and methods of control both financial and otherwise including risk analysis and risk management; and for ensuring the charity is complying with all aspects of the law, relevant regulations and good practice.

Composition and reporting
- The audit committee will consist of no fewer than [number] trustees appointed by the board, the external auditor, and others with appropriate skills expertise of whom at least [number] are external and independent of the charity/VCO.
- The board will appoint the Chair of the audit committee.
- Any trustee may attend a meeting of the audit committee, including those who are not members of the audit committee.
- The Chief Executive, the finance director, director of operations, internal auditor and such other members of staff as the chair may require shall be in attendance at meetings.
- Until otherwise determined by the board of trustees, a quorum shall consists of [number] members of the committee.
- Members of the audit committee may serve for not more than [number] years.
- The audit committee will report back regularly, and at least every [number] months to the board of trustees.
- The audit committee is authorised to obtain appropriate external legal and other professional advice in order to fulfil its responsibility to the board of trustees.
- The audit committee is authorised to investigate on the behalf on the board of trustees anything that threatens or adversely affects the accomplishment of the charity's/VCO's aims and objectives, its assets, the reliability of all records and information, and its compliance with all relevant laws, regulations, policies and its governing instruments.

Main duties

General

- To recommend to the board of trustees a framework of effective audit coverage, having reviewed the internal and external audit processes;
- To advise the board of trustees on the minimum and optimum level of internal and external audit arrangements;
- To ensure that regular audits are carried out in the following areas: legal, risk, financial (including statutory annual audits, VAT, PAYE, procurement, payments and contracts), health and safety, investments and insurance, and to contribute to these reviews;
- To monitor internal and external audit reviews and to advise the board of trustees accordingly. (This may be by means of summary reports from the Chief Executive or internal auditor ensuring that the full reports are available to any member of the audit committee or the trustee board should they require to see them.);
- To investigate on behalf of the board any financial or administrative matter which may put the charity/VCO at risk;
- To examine reports on special investigations and to advise the board of trustees accordingly;
- To consider the appropriateness of executive action following internal audit reviews and to advise senior management on any additional or alternative steps to be taken;
- To ensure there is coordination and good working relationships between internal audit, external audit and any other review bodies that have been set up;
- To encourage a culture within the charity/VCO whereby each individual feels that he or she has a part to play in guarding the probity of the charity/VCO, and is able to take any concerns or worries to an appropriate member of the management team or in exceptional circumstances directly to the chair of the audit committee;
- To provide minutes of all audit committee meetings for review at meetings of the board of trustees;
- Effectiveness of internal financial controls and risk management arrangements;
- Security of assets including an asset register.

External audits

- To determine the frequency of tendering for external auditing services;
- To consider tenders for the external auditing services and recommend to the board of trustees which firm should carry out the annual external audit of the charity's/VCO's statutory accounts;
- To scrutinise and advise the board on the contents of the draft audit report and of any management letter that the auditors may wish to present to the board, and to formulate for board use any written representations that may be needed by the auditors in connection with the charity's/VCO's statutory accounts or any other financial statements;
- To discuss with the external auditors any problems or reservations arising from the draft external audit report and draft management letter, reporting relevant issues back to the board, and advising the board accordingly;
- To review the performance of the charity's/VCO's auditors and advise the board on any changes that ought to be made to their terms of engagement;
- To obtain any necessary external professional advice to enable the audit committee to carry out its responsibilities more effectively.

External audits

All charities or VCOs with an income exceeding £250,000 are required by law to have an annual audit from a registered external auditor. (Note: the new Charities Act recommends relating thresholds solely to income and raising this limit to £500,000. See the Charity Commission website for updates.) The purpose of an audit is to provide independent confirmation of the financial affairs of an organisation. The auditor will be required to express the opinion that the accounts give a 'true and fair' view. As well as commenting on the accounts, the auditors should also review the trustees' report.

Many organisations have an audit committee to oversee external audits among other duties. Typically an influential committee member or even Chair of this committee, the Treasurer has an important role to play in managing the audit process through this group. (Note: If there is no audit committee, the panel providing oversight should include the Treasurer, Chief Executive and at least one other trustee.)

Choosing an auditor

Appointment of suitable auditors for an organisation is essential and is normally carried out by the finance or audit committee, as appropriate, with the appointment announced at the AGM. The organisation should put the audit out to tender on a regular basis – ideally every three years – with existing auditors automatically invited to apply.

To find external auditors, look for advertisements in mainstream sector publications including *Charity Finance* magazine Once a year this magazine also publishes a league table of external auditors showing which organisations they work with. The Charity Finance Directors' Group publication, Charity Finance Yearbook, regularly includes a gazetteer of reputable audit firms. For more information, see *Resources*.

Briefing the auditor

It is vital that the auditor knows the organisation and understands fully what its mandate and mission is. To make sure the audit runs smoothly, hold a planning meeting attended by the auditors, audit committee and DOF. Use this meeting to iron out practical details, such as what documents are to be prepared ready for the audit.

This meeting has additional importance for charities incorporated under the Companies Acts due to the new statutory disclosure now required in the Directors' Report (Trustees' Annual Report).

The auditor will also need to know whether they are just to do an audit or provide additional services. At the planning meeting, discuss additional services such as drafting accounts, taxation services including PAYE and VAT returns and management consultancy services to help with specific problems. Record the minutes of this meeting and distribute afterwards to attendees. Following the meeting, summarise decisions in a written brief to the auditors.

The audit should cover five key areas:

- factors affecting auditor's assessment of risk;
- analysis of relevant law and regulations;
- controls over key aspects of a organisation's income and assets;
- matters to be reported directly to the Charity Commission;
- content of report on financial statements.

Presenting the management letter

The management letter is prepared by the auditor to deliver the results of the audit. Addressed to the board, it sets out any concerns the auditor may have about financial controls and other matters, and seeks assurances, where necessary, to supplement their audit findings.

The management letter is regarded as confidential between the auditor and the board of trustees. The Treasurer plays an important role in presenting the management letter to the board and helping trustees interpret its significance. The Treasurer should be involved in a meeting with the auditors to go through the management letter in detail in preparation for introducing the findings to the board.

Independent examinations

By law, small non-company charitable organisations with an income or total expenditure of under £250, 000 can choose (except where their Governing Document requires an audit) to conduct an independent examination of their accounts rather than a formal audit. (Note: this threshold is under review in the new Charities Act, which proposes to make independent examination an option for organisations with an income of £500,000 or less. See the Charity Commission website for the latest information on the progress of Charities Act.)

The role of the Treasurer during an independent examination is similar to his or her involvement in a full audit. Indeed, in many cases the audit or finance committee is given the brief of working with the independent examiner in much the same way it works with an auditor: providing a brief, selecting and preparing the examiner, acting as liaison for the organisation, receiving and reviewing the report and making recommendations on actions to the board.

In small organisations with no formal committee, the Treasurer him- or herself may have the task of working with the independent examiner on behalf of the board. In either case, the person or group overseeing the independent examination process should be familiar with the Charity Commission's detailed guidelines on conducting an independent examination CC63: *Independent examination of charity accounts*, available in print and on the internet. See *Resources* for details.

Trustee boards look to the Treasurer to guide them through some of the most important and demanding financial oversight tasks from budgeting to responding to an internal audit. Good practice notes on key areas provides an introduction to several of the most significant areas of interest to the Treasurer. It offers an overview of key financial functions, such as preparing and presenting management accounts, managing external and internal audits, serving on the audit committee and dealing with statutory reporting. Plus it provides of wealth of tips, pointers and good advice for Treasurers as they help the board accomplish the vital tasks that secure the organisation from risk. Finally, a detailed Resources section helps Treasurers and those who work with them find out further information and get support.

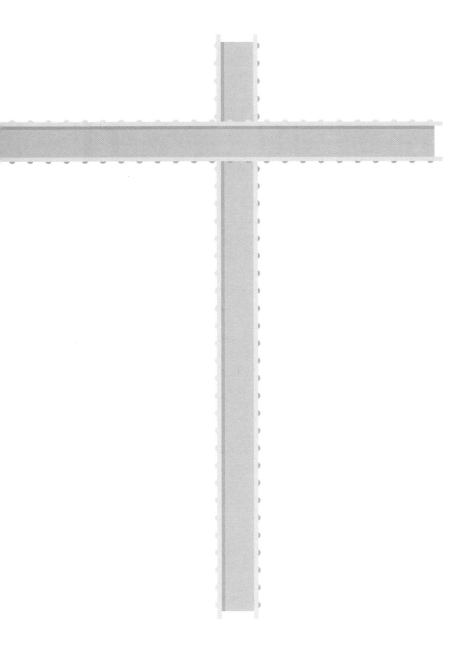

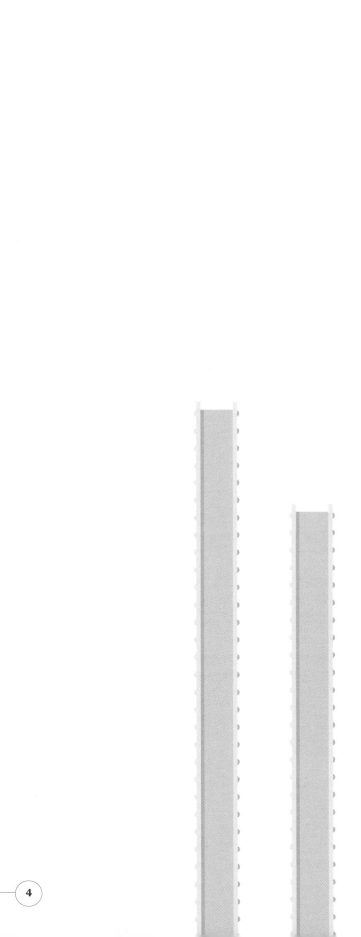

The examination process

An independent examination is not a full professional audit but more of a high level review by a suitably qualified professional, where appropriate. It covers slightly less than a full audit but is still a very thorough form of scrutiny. Its aim is to ensure that accounts are correct and systems adequate for the organisation's needs. An independent examiner will:

- look at the accounts;
- develop an understanding of the organisational context;
- compare the accounts to the books;
- perform other needed checks;
- write an independent report for circulation with the accounts.

The examiner is required:

- To follow the directions set out in the Charity Commission's guidance, CC63: Independent Examination of Charity Accounts;
- To obtain a proper understanding of the organisation, including the governing document and methods of working: mechanically examining the books is not sufficient;
- To be able to identify material transactions that might represent a breach of trust;
- To establish whether the organisation has maintained proper accounting records as required by section 41 of the Charities Act 1993;
- In extreme cases where the examiner believes that a member of staff or trustee has been involved in 'deliberate or reckless misconduct in the administration' of the organisation, he or she must inform the Charity Commission directly;
- To provide a written report that will be attached to the accounts. This report is directed to the trustees but is a public document.

Finding an examiner

An examiner does not necessarily need to have accounting qualifications, but Charity Commission guidelines recommend that organisations with an income of over £100,000 choose an examiner who is, at least, a trained accountant. For more details on selecting an examiner, see Charity Commission guidelines CC63: Independent Examination of Charity Accounts. For more information on independent examinations and a list of qualified examiners, contact the Association of Charity Independent Examiners (ACIE). See Resources for contact details.

Internal audits

The purpose of an internal audit is to carry out an independent appraisal of the effectiveness of the policies, procedures and standards and, above all, to help organisations deal systematically with risk. Recent research by groups such as the Institute of Chartered Secretaries and Administrators (ICSA) and the Institute for Internal Auditors (IIA) shows that organisations benefit from regular internal audits.

Internal auditors work with trustees and management to ensure that all major risks are identified and analysed on a regular basis and that appropriate measures are taken to minimise risk to the organisation. Internal audits bring perspective, providing insight into what happens in other organisations and striving to offer a detached view of the organisation and its activities. Internal auditors can contribute much to the assessment of risk in all its forms: external threats to the organisation, potential dangers inherent in particular services and processes, and the risk involved in projects to be undertaken. The audit results should most importantly contain information on how best to minimise the likelihood and the impact of risk.

Another area of importance for internal audit is the review of controls. Traditionally such a review starts with financial controls (see below) but it should also cover areas such as operations, IT, communications and fraud. Risk assessments should be updated annually and the responses to the risks changed as appropriate when risks change.

Choosing an internal auditor

There are a number of aspects to take into consideration when selecting internal auditors. Boards should take into account the nature of the organisation and try to choose auditors with the skills to form an overall picture of organisational risks and systems. The governing body must determine what they want the audit to achieve, then use that brief to select the auditors most likely to deliver results.

Internal auditors should preferably be independent of the organisation's finance function, therefore it is vital they have access to the board and Chief Executive. Many organisations use their standing audit committees for this task but refresh their mandate with a brief that specifically covers the internal audit. The Treasurer in this case will have the responsibility of giving feedback to the board.

Further advice can be sought from the Charities Internal Audit Network (CIAN). This group has the active support of the Charity Commission and the IIA. The aim of CIAN is to assist its members in the effective discharge of their responsibilities and to promote the profession of internal audit in the voluntary sector, thereby helping organisations to achieve their objectives more efficiently. For more information, see *Resources*.

Managing financial controls

The Treasurer has an important role in helping the board set up effective financial control systems for monitoring and recording. Such controls are essential in helping to show potential donors and beneficiaries that an organisation's property is safeguarded and efficiently managed. Having sufficiently rigorous controls not only provides protection for the organisation's assets but is also the best defence against a charge of failing to protect funds and being in breach of trust. Trustees – particularly the Treasurer – are responsible for making sure these controls exist.

Effective monitoring can be difficult for trustees who don't work in the organisation full time or see day-to-day operations. By necessity, trustees must delegate controls to trusted individuals inside the organisation. With his or her knowledge of finance, the Treasurer can help the board find the right level of delegation as authorised by the organisation's governing document (or section 11 of the Trustee Act 2000). Even when controls are delegated, trustees need to be sure that systems and procedures are in place to enable them to check that controls are in force and are functioning correctly. Here again, the Treasurer can advise on what indicators will be significant.

Trustees have a legal duty to exercise such skill and care as is reasonable in the circumstances when making delegations and when determining the extent of the delegation. They also have a legal duty to review the arrangements under which the delegation has been made and oversee how these arrangements have been put into effect; this includes considering the need for giving the persons delegated directions as to the exercise of their functions, revising the terms of the delegation and terminating the delegation.

Reporting checklist

The Treasurer must guide and advise the trustee board as it fulfils its reporting duties for the organisation.

Charity Commission

- File accounts and Annual Return: the deadline is ten months after year end although early filing is recommended
- File the Summary Information Return (organisations with an income of £1 million or more)
- Manage investigations
- File trustees' appointment/registration forms

Companies House

- File accounts and Annual Return
- File directors' appointment/resignation forms

Inland Revenue

- File tax returns on time
- Pay NI and PAYE on time
- Respond to queries

Customs and Excise

- Maintain accurate VAT records
- File VAT returns on time
- Respond to queries

General

- Preserve all documentary and supporting information
- Keep all records for required amount of time

Other areas of importance

Investments

The new Trustee Act 2000 gave trustees wider powers of investment but the markets are now more volatile. Ethical or socially responsible investment over the past few years has come into prominence. Many organisations have investment sub-committees made up of trustees and independent experts: the Treasurer must play a role in all this.

Pensions

This is an important area for many organisations especially for those with final pension salaried schemes. Pension rules are changing all the time and regulation has greatly increased. The Treasurer needs to keep up with changing rules and must be a member of any pension sub committee.

Risk assessment

Risk management is important for all organisations. The organisation must define the major risks and plan how to deal with them. This needs to be reported to trustees annually and must be included in trustees report and accounts.

The Treasurer has an important role to play in the management of risk. Trustees have to make a disclosure in the accounts regarding their review of risks and the systems in place to minimise them. Treasurers should ensure that risks are assessed, a risk register is in place and the management of risk permeates the culture of their organisation. The Treasurer should also ensure that trustees review risks at least once a year.

Reserves

The Treasurer must be involved in the development of the reserves policy and should assume the trustee guardianship role for the maintenance and development of reserves. The policy has to be reported on and reviewed each year.

Key performance indicators

There are currently pressures on organisations to improve the way they measure the outcomes and impacts of their work. SORP 2005, the Summary Information Return (SIR) and GuideStar are all pushing organisations in the direction of greater accountability. This can be a challenge for organisations but the Treasurer can adopt a leading role in promoting the establishment of good measuring systems.

The first step for Treasurers is to develop an understanding of measurement. There is a lot of technical jargon on the subject but most of it can be simply explained as follows:

- **Activities:** what the organisation does such as training courses or counselling sessions for people seeking work.

- **Outputs:** the 'countable' units of the activities, for example the number of training courses run or the number of counselling sessions.

- **Outcomes:** the effect on the beneficiaries: e.g. how many of the people are employed.

- **Impacts:** the longer-term effects on the beneficiaries including both direct and indirect effects, for example how long this person remains in employment, his or her career path and the overall effect on his or her life.

Resources

African and Caribbean Diversity (ACD)
An organisation for promoting diversity with links to African and Caribbean individuals with financial expertise.

ACD
Suite 34 Delta House
175-177 Borough High Street
London SE1 1HR
020 7939 9975
info@acdiversity.org
www.acff.org

Association of Charity Independent Examiners (ACIE)
Promoting high standards among independent examiners.

ACIE
Bentley Resource Centre
High Street
Bentley
Doncaster
01302 828 338
info@acie.org.uk
www.acie.org.uk

Centre for Charity Effectiveness
The Centre for Charity Effectiveness offers consultancy, mentoring, learning networks, courses and degrees for those working in the voluntary sector. Its curriculum includes courses and a degree in voluntary sector finance and financial management.

Centre for Charity Effectiveness
106 Bunhill Row
London EC1Y 8TZ
020 7040 8667
centreforcharityeffectiveness@city.ac.org
www.centreforcharityeffectiveness.org

Charity Commission
The latest in regulation and advice for voluntary sector finance. Check regularly for new publications and online updates.

Charity Commission
Charity Commission Direct
PO Box 1227
Liverpool L69 3UG 0845 300 0218
Hearing impaired 0845 300 0219
enquiries@charitycommission.gsi.gov.uk
www.charitycommission.gov.uk

Charity Finance Director's Group (CFDG)
An organisation which supports all aspects of voluntary sector finance offering information, networking and training, including finance and investment training for trustees.

CFDG
3rd Floor
Downstream Building
1, London Bridge
London SE1 9BG
www.cfdg.org.uk

Charities Internal Audit Network (CIAN)
Networking, seminars, workshops and training for all those who carry out internal audits, free and available to anyone.

CIAN (internet only)
www.cianonline.org.uk
enquiries@cianonline.org.uk

European Federation of Black Women Business Owners (EFBWBO)
A source of black finance professionals willing to serve on voluntary sector boards.

EFBWBO
16 Trinity Gardens
London SW9 8DP
www.blackwomeninbusiness.com
info@efbwbo.net

The Finance Hub
The Finance Hub offers advice and information in many areas of finance.

The Finance Hub
St. Andrew's House
18-20 St. Andrew Street
London EC4A 3AY
020 7832 3016
www.financehub.org.uk

Honorary Treasurer's Forum
Established by Treasurers and accountancy professionals, the Honorary Treasurer's Forum organises seminars, networking events and publications designed to support the important work of Treasurers in VCOs.

Honorary Treasurer's Forum
c/o L.D. Jones, OBE
The Clock House
231 Kentwood Hill
Tilehurst
Reading RG31 6JD
0118 941 2365
ldjones1000@aol.com

Institute of Chartered Secretaries and Administrators (ICSA)
Promotes high standards in systems and governance. Useful publications on many aspects of voluntary sector work.

ICSA
16 Park Crescent
London W1B 1AH
020 7580 4741
info@icsa.co.uk
www.icsa.org.uk

Institute of Internal Auditors UK and Ireland
Information, networking and training for internal auditors.

IIA UK and Ireland
13 Abbeville Mews
88 Clapham Park Road
London SW4 7BX
020 7498 0101
info@iia.org.uk
www.iia.org.uk

National Council for Voluntary Organisations (NCVO)

Advice, events and information on all aspects of voluntary sector finance and governance including internal and external audits, risk and controls. Online, follow the links to Finance.

NCVO
Regent's Wharf
8 All Saints Street
London NW1 9RL
020 7713 6161
ncvo@ncvo-vol.org.uk
www.ncvo-vol.org.uk

Office of the Scottish Charities Regulator (OSCR)

Guidance and information for VCOs in Scotland.

OSCR
2nd Floor
Quadrant House
9 Riverside Drive
Dundee
DD1 4NY
013 8222 0446
info@oscr.org.uk
www.oscr.org.uk

Public Concern at Work (PCaW)

Public Concern at Work offers advice and support for individuals and organisations setting up whistleblowing procedures or dealing with cases of whistleblowing.

PCaW
Suite 301
16 Baldwins Gardens
London EC1N 7RJ
020 7404 6609
whistle@pcaw.co.uk
www.pcaw.co.uk

Voluntary and Community Unit of the Department for Social Development for Northern Ireland
Guidance and advice for VCOs in Northern Ireland

Voluntary and Community Development Unit
Department for Social Development, Northern Ireland
Lighthouse Building
1 Cromac Place
Gasworks Business Park
Ormeau Road
Belfast BT7 2JB
028 9082 9425
www.dsdni.gov.uk